NOTHING IS OKAY

NOTHING IS OKAY

by Rachel Wiley

"I fall in love with myself, and I want someone to share it with me. And I want someone to share me, with me."

—EARTHA KITT

||||||||||

Published by Button Poetry / Exploding Pinecone Press
Minneapolis, MN 55403 | http://www.buttonpoetry.com

||||||||||

Manufactured in the United States of America

Cover Design: Amy Law

ISBN 978-1-943735-30-3

TABLE OF CONTENTS

BUT THEY SAY I WILL NOT MAKE IT

When you are fat (and I am fat) the streets are full of
soothsayers
telling you how you will die.
    They all seem so anxious for my heart
    like it's an unattended package at the airport
  so I move thru the world listening
    for my heart like it must be a clock
      swallowed by a crocodile.
                     No,
          a canary that goes silent much too late.
          No,
they are certain it is going to attack, my heart,
      like a hungry bear on a camp ground
        ripping a zipper down my chest, cracking
      my sternum like a cheap tent pole.
          No,
      I am not at all sorry for my size
  so I must be a barge which would make my heart a fish
          washed onto the deck
      GaspingFloppingSlamming scales off its body
    like an angry beauty queen ripping sequins from a dress
        that didn't sparkle enough to win
    but then that would make my heart a beauty queen
that can't walk in heels...
          No,
            wait.
      My heart is an hourglass filled with gunpowder
    and at any given moment some wild spark
        is gonna blow me sky high
 so, I don't know, maybe this is why I love the way I do
    with teeth and swallow and song and snarl
      and water and sparkle and consequence
    maybe this is why I show up to your front door
      out of breath and full of dazzle
        like this is the last ballyhoo
 and nothing at all can wait till the morning.

Forgive me, they keep telling me that my heart is not my heart.
They keep telling me that I am dying.
This may be our last chance.

REJECTION #1

Dear MrTongueRing69,

Thank you for your submission, however we were unable to read it as our office is not currently equipped with a way-back machine to travel to an era when your screen name was clever and probably somewhat alluring. I can only assume it read something like "A/S/L?" before launching into the screech-and-click dial-up-modem siren song of your people.

Nonetheless, it is probably still safe to wish you well in finding a home for your cock.

Kindest Regards,
Nothing is Ok, Cupid Quarterly

MIXED GIRL

After Angel Nafis and Terrance Hayes

Mixed Girl, White Mother
Mixed Girl, Black Father
Yes, really
Mixed Girl, White Mother's Hair
       Black Father's Lips
       patient while you pick and choose
       what's exotic enough
       sighs thru tired jokes about how she only gets half of
       Martin Luther King Day off work
       White Mother's Guilt
       Black Father's Survival
       Survivor's Guilt
       Passing
       wonders if it's called passing because something dies inside
each time
       carries her blackness like Peter Pan's shadow shot down and
       stitched desperately back to her heels
Mixed Girl also Fat
Yes, Fat
Fat, Mixed Girl reconciled the word Fat
       passes slowly, a heavy drop of water
       passes race but not weight limits
       sighs thru tired jokes about black men loving fat white
women
       living punchline
Fat, Mixed Girl also Queer
Yes, Really
Queer, Fat, Mixed Girl's pronouns are
She/Her/Your Majesty
       femme
       triple threat invisible
       double agents as Straight Shameful White Lady
       sighs thru tired jokes about greed
       as sexual orientation
       admits to having mostly had relationships

with cis-men
no less attracted to women tho
no less attracted to non-binary beauty tho
probably thinks you're cute
probably wants to make out with you
Yes, you
Queer, Fat, Mixed Girl is a Feminist
No shit.
Yes, Feminist
Feminist, Queer, Fat, Mixed Girl is full body intersection
passing whiteness, passing straightness,
passing weakness
makes her a conceal carry revolt
has one common enemy
aims to gut the white supremacist patriarchy
rouge her cheeks with his blood

Feminist
Queer
Fat
Mixed
Girl
knows he will
never
ever
see her
coming

MY WHITENESS HITS ON ME IN A BAR

You're welcome.
You hear me?
I said you're welcome
for those eyes
like your mother's
stolen sapphires
when you could've had your father's mud puddles.
You're welcome.
They make you look so innocent
so trusting.
Don't forget I got you that troubleless hair too
The same hair that got you a good job
or at least didn't keep you from one.
You really should be more grateful.
Your skin is default nude
default skin tone.
No one assumes you are uneducated.
I do that.
For you.
For Us.
All of us.
This ruling race of us.
Which is better than them.
Which deserves more than them.
Is it so hard to show a little gratitude?
It's a compliment.
The way the cops won't doubt you/press your face into the dirt.
The way bullets won't hunt your light skin/your pink cheeks.
The way I built this place a bomb shelter for you.
Stop fighting for some part of you no one can see/wants to see.
Stop fighting for people that don't look like you.
You got real lucky, girl.
Don't you feel lucky?
Don't you love the way I've made all of this easy for you?
You should show me how much you love it.
Show me with those colored-girl lips you ended up with.

Kneel for me like you're scrubbing a floor—I know
you know how.
That's in your blood.
I haven't forgotten that you pass.
Maybe you forgot that I am the one who crowned you
queen of the paper bag prom
but that can be our little secret.
All you have to do is relax
and let it happen.

THE ART OF RIDING A TANDEM BIKE ALONE

In the Museum of Broken Relationships
there is a living diorama
a real and breathing spinster in bloom
coated in cat hair and cynicism.
Watch, as she cooks dinner for one and eats it over the sink.
Be amazed, as she ages alone save of course the cat
(who is just as cantankerous as she).
Behold, how she drinks bourbon straight from the bottle
because it offers her a mouth to kiss.
Witness, how she weeps until she dissolves
and then wakes up to rebuild herself
one salt grain at a time the next morning.
Observe, the cavernous sigh as she realizes it will all have to be done
again
and again
and again...
See the actual butterflies from her very stomach
which once danced with possibility
pinned by their wings.
Feast your eyes, on this true human rest stop.
A motel that dreamed once of becoming a home
silly temporary thing with soap-sliver hands
and a body/a bed that held lovers as though
they might actually stay.

IN THE EVENT THE WIND IS KNOCKED OUT OF YOU

Remember that this chest grasp
this violent sigh
this exodus is temporary
nothing more than a spasm
though the force that knocked
it from you, the weight that
dipped you to the dirt,
the vortex kiss that put
you on your back
may leave some welt
or knot or void,
the air will return.
Trust the bone nest cradling
your pink precious lungs
to mother the breath
back home to you
and also, to expand wide enough
to sob or to sing
or to just resume.

COOKING WITH TEARS

Because nothing brings a meal together quite like the right seasoning, what better seasoning than TEARS?

Our very own tear ducts are the salt shakers of the face, so go ahead, tap into that sadness and cry over your meals for a truly nostalgic flavor sensation.

Who among us doesn't have fond childhood memories of Mom weeping over a hot stove top occasionally muttering about lost dreams before telling us *everything is just fine* before sending us outside to play until dinner? You can keep the tradition alive, even if just for yourself since you have failed in your womanly obligation to reproduce and your grandmother keeps hinting that it really would be fine if you are a lesbian.

These days, synthetic tears are available for people who might be worried about their sadness intake but still crave the robust flavor of tears just like Mother used to make. As with most healthy substitutes, you will be sacrificing some flavor, but you can't have it both ways.

When throwing dinner parties, it may be important to remember that some of your guests may have removed tears from their diets due to the effect on the planet or some such nonsense (and despite the fact that not everyone has access to organic fair trade happiness) so it may be necessary to prepare a no-tears option to please all of your guests.

After all, isn't pleasing others what life's all about?

FEMME VISIBILITY

My queerness
is not unlike
a cat on a leash.
It's awkward
people don't always understand why it's happening
or how it works
but it's not hurting anyone
so it goes mostly unbothered.

The difference
is that you can see
a cat
on a leash.

NOTES ON DEPRESSION

I.

I have clawed my way to *okay* and it will
just have to do for now.
I sent my body out ahead of me, a guide line tied to her foot
hold her above me
a sullen balloon woman.
I wait to see how many scars she returns with before deciding
whether to join the world whole
or to leave her to sway with the wind and seem at peace
a distraction, while I tunnel out.

II.

My latest hobby is screaming.
I scream into things.
It was just pillows at first,
now it is anything I think can hold my trauma.

I have haunted the whole house.

III.

There was a brilliant surprise party here 3 months ago. I have been
unable to bring myself to toss out the wilted balloons or to sweep up
the confetti. I didn't want it to end. A celebration is just a way of
begging the good things to stay. A false promise that we could always
be just like this, a false promise worth clinging to, worth living in the
aftermath of.

A PLAGUE OF DOUBTS

Maybe, if I did not

try so hard
panic so often
flinch so easily
enjoy the attention from the married men
fuck the man with the girlfriend every time
he calls
like the God-feeling of that balloon boy's
heart under my heel
insist on standing up for myself
choose my work over them
need so much alone time
leave the church
give it up on the first date
make them wait so long
cry in front of them
look so mean
tell them I need them
need them
ignore the red flags
search for the red flags in silence
try to save them despite my own undertow
compare this one to the last one
compromise so little
compromise so much
take them at their word
give them mine
show off the scars
miss the bus
try to convince myself it is not real
stay when I could still leave
know my worth
talk so loud
have so many feelings
want it so badly
keep looking for it
expect it—

everyone keeps saying it happens when you least do

HOW TO EAT YOUR FEELINGS: ANGER

You will need:

    -2 to 3 boxes of Klondike Bars any flavor
    -1 jar of Nutella
    -1 polar bear costume

Build an igloo around your head out of Klondike bars using Nutella
as a bonding agent.
Pretend you are a polar bear.
Eat your head free.
Release the rage.

Feeds:
One Very Angry Polar Bear

GLORY IN TWO PARTS

What you think you mean when you say that I Glorify Obesity
is that I am an undeserved celebration,
a gluttonous mass of unrepent,
a patron saint of unhealth,
a pageant of sloth and wheeze and uncontrol,
a gasping-heart Madonna.
You think you mean: how can she possibly raise her fat face
to the sun in worship
rather than submitting to the gravity of shame?
that I am a sickness rolled in caramel and body glitter
a fatted golden calf in a sugar-glazed crown,
that my very existence blesses other massive bodies
begs them to drink from a chalice of my toxic blood
and melts dignity into hot spit on their tongues.
What you think you mean when you say that I Glorify Obesity is,
How dare she.

What you actually mean when you say that I Glorify Obesity
is that indeed I am Glorious
because who would not exalt something
as miracle as a living body?
You mean to say that I carry this body
every day like a sacrament
to revere the way I keep rising despite a world
who does not want the truth of me.
You mean to say that I am a cup runneth over
that my walk preaches a gospel of rubbing thighs
that my arm fat jiggles a pair of fleshy tambourines
that my ass sways like a well-trained choir
that my fupa is an altar built around something holy
and worth bowing down to.
Now, you can be the devil I dance away or you can dance
your devils away with me.
Hating me will not absolve you of your own shameful
sins against the body
and I will not carry them on my back either.

I will just be a one-woman tent revival
with the lights on late
sweat-slick and handing out glory.
What you actually mean when you say that I Glorify Obesity
is *Hallelujah.*
So go ahead and say *Hallelujah.*
Say Hallelujah to the back fat
Hallelujah to the generous rolls of flesh
Hallelujah to the cellulite
Hallelujah to the stretch marks
Hallelujah to the still-thumping heart.
Sing it to the rafters.
Glory Glory
glory
glory

HALLOWEEN SHOPPING WITH MY NIECE

Do you want to be a kitty cat?

No.

a princess?

I'm already a princess.

Of course you are.
Oh look, you could be a slice of pizza!

Nahh...

Do you want to be Doc McStuffins?!

I want to be something super scary!

But, Doc McStuffins is terrifying to the Patriarchy.

What's a patriarchy? Sounds like a kind of dinosaur?

Yes, Darling, the Patriarchy IS a dinosaur.

*Is it a very big dinosaur? Cause I could be a bigger one.
I could be a dinosaur that eats a patriarchy.*

GRIEF

Written from a prompt by Siaara Freeman

Grief is my stern-mouthed mother,
though people swear we must be sisters
the way I age with every loss.
It's in the eyes, they say.
She has come again
to dote on me
since my love has gone.
She shows up unannounced and never alone.
She comes swinging a bird cage with a cockatoo named Bargaining
perched inside.
It repeats everything I say back to me minus the question marks.
Depression is my father.
He demands that I carry him from room to room
while he haunts my house with deep slow sighs.
Anger is a territorial child in a dirty party dress and scuffed patent
leather shoes
looking for things to break
while my spinster aunt, Denial, stands in the front yard humming
Didn't We Almost Have It All.
She never comes inside on the off-chance Love is coming back.

I feed them whatever I happen to have in the freezer.
It is an unthawed bounty of lonesome
an entire wedding cake minus the groom
plastic bags of changed locks and apartment keys
the other halves of all the dinners I have ever taken
the time to lovingly cook
only to eat my portion alone over the kitchen sink
a brick of foil-wrapped anniversaries uncelebrated
a cold-cut spread of photographs and love letters.

When every stomach has been fed,
when at last we are full and numb-mouthed from feasting on freezer-
burnt wanting,
when Grief is dozing off in front of the nightly news,

and Bargaining is building a nest of newspaper obituaries,
when Depression lays whiskey-sick and snoring
across the couch
and Anger has tantrumed herself into a fitful sleep
under the dinner table,

my grandmother, Acceptance, who stores promises in the deep
creases of her brow, hands me a dish towel to dry each plate and
platter that she washes until they sparkle like new again.

AN INCOMPLETE PINTEREST BOARD OF USES FOR THE ABUNDANCE OF CONDOMS THAT EXPIRED AFTER HE LEFT

-Dish mittens! (like dish gloves, except not)

-Learn to make balloon animals for the neighborhood kids

-Donate them to an up-and-coming drug cartel for filling with heroin and transporting

-Rainboots for the cat

-Throw them into a bowl of not-yet-expired condoms and play a fun game of condom roulette (aka whoopsie baby)

-Fill them with your spinster tears and throw them at happy couples

-Covers for the bananas, zucchini, cucumbers, and other oblong fruits and veggies

-Cut them length-wise, dry them in the sun, and sew them together to make a protective sofa cover.

-Sell them on Etsy as "infinity change purses"

-Sleeping bags for caterpillars

-Just write new dates on them and hope for the best

-Draw faces on them and use them as finger puppets to re-enact all the moments that went wrong in your last relationship and snapchat them to your ex

-Keep rolled-up copies of all your inevitable restraining orders safe and dry in them

HOROSCOPE FOR THE PREMATURE SCORPIO: MARCH 2013

That Libra is your Diego Rivera.

When you can hear your ex fucking the next-door neighbor thru your shared bedroom wall, find a new lover and fuck louder. If a dance partner is not readily available without settling (as you are no longer permitted to settle), buy a new vibrator and make him jealous of you and you alone. Permit yourself to make the sounds he could never elicit from you. Make him jealous of the way he cannot feel whole without you the way you can feel whole without him. The way you can wear empty hands like a new trend that he simply cannot pull off. Stop mourning. He will never be over you. He will be ungrateful and distracted but he will never have it so good. Karma, it's petty that way. You love him as you have always loved him but you will die first and cannot wait for him to catch up. If he misses the rendezvous point, you go on without him.

Lucky numbers: his birthday, his new lover's birthday and the next full moon.

INCANTATION FOR AUTONOMY

And so, I whisper into scorched grass
a call to all of the witches burned for being feral bodies.

I beg you to show yourselves in the fireplaces
of congressional figures who make choices against the autonomy of
these righteous bodies that cradle a uterus.

Scream something unholy thru the pilot lights of their furnaces.
Haunt the warmth of their existence with a raving and
howling hunger they cannot possibly feed.

First, each man who aims to carve an orphanage of cribs from our hip
bones; provoke him to strip naked in the center of town, account for
every blemish on his holy flesh.

And then, dance wild and naked in the prayer candles
of every goody woman who robs choice from our mouths.

Drive her into the river to prove she can sink
gracefully as only a truly righteous woman would.

Come dear witches, remind them of what we can do
when our bodies are used as evidence for our undoing.

FAT JOKE

The old joke goes:
Patient walks into the doctor's office and says, "Doctor, it hurts when
I move my arm like this, what should I do?" and the doctor says, "So,
don't move your arm like that."

Now,

Fat Girl walks into the doctor's office and says, "Doctor, it hurts
when I move my arm like this, what should I do?" and the doctor
says, "Have you considered weight loss surgery?"
Fat Girl walks into the doctor's office for a flu shot
and gets a lecture about BMI
Fat Girl walks into the doctor's office for an earache and gets asked if
she's ever eaten a salad
Fat Girl walks into the doctor's office with a spider bite and the
doctor obsesses over how low her blood pressure is—low for such a
fat person anyway—and insists on checking it 3 times before he
believes it, has to be reminded of the purple mass of throbbing spider
venom that brought her here in the first place
Fat Girl walks into the doctor's office to ask about antidepressants
and gets prescribed exercise instead
Fat Girl walks into the doctor's office for a standard 3-month followup
appointment and the doctor says, "Have you considered weight
loss surgery?"
Fat Girl gets tired of only ever being diagnosed fat
so Fat Girl stops walking into the doctor's office

Fat Girl walks to the store
and has insults flicked at her like still-lit
cigarettes from passing cars
Fat Girl walks onto a crowded bus and stands because she does not
wish to share a seat and make anyone else uncomfortable

Fat Girl logs onto the internet, gets comments from keyboard doctors
that claim concern for her health
suggests crash diets

suggests flat-tummy tea
suggests diet pills that would stop fat girl's heart but fat girl will have
died trying to get thin
Fat Girl walks into the world and says,
"World, it hurts to exist like this."
World says, "So stop existing like that"
World says, "Have you considered weight loss surgery?"
would rather she slice herself open than to exist as she does
side effects be damned
Despite all of this, Fat Girl still manages to love her fat body
World says, "Stop glorifying obesity."
Fat Girl walks up to World, says, "I do not owe you shrinking, you
know. I do not owe you thinness, attempted thinness, or desired
thinness because you assume thinness equals health. I do not owe you
health, perceived or otherwise, to receive basic respect. I am
deserving of existence. I am deserving of care. I am deserving of first
no harm done."
World says,
"That is the best joke we've heard all day."

POTENTIAL SLOGANS FOR OKCUPID

OkCupid: Who Knew You Could Be So Disinterested in SO Many People?!

OkCupid: Because Otherwise You'll Die Alone and the Cat Will Eat Your Eyeballs Like Fruit Cups

OkCupid: Because You Overbought Condoms and They Expire in a Week

OkCupid: Because You Didn't Want an Orgasm Anyway

OkCupid: Got Shame? Want Some?

OkCupid: Because Hope Is for 20-Year-Olds

OkCupid: Helping Married Couples Proposition Bisexuals for Threesomes Since 2001

OkCupid: An Online Catalog for Hate Fucking

OkCupid: We Literally Don't Know What A Clitoris Is!!

OkCupid: We Literally Don't Care What A Clitoris Is!!

OkCupid: All of the Dick Pics Without Any of the Hassle of Actually Wanting Them

OkCupid: Because Dating Should Be Like Picking a Scab

OkCupid: Helping to Keep Boxed Wine Sales up Since 2004

OkCupid: All the Motivation You Need to Take Back Your Terrible Ex in One Place

OkCupid: Come for the Boredom, Stay Because You Are Literally Out of Options.

REJECTION #2

Dear MrMan1980,

Thank you for your submission: *wanna see my cock?!*

Unfortunately, we are not accepting Flash Fiction at this time.
Please check with us again in 6 months when our standards have
dropped or perhaps when one of our exes gets engaged again and we
are eating icing straight from the tub while wearing our prom dress.
Best of luck in finding a home for your cock.

Kindest Regards,
Nothing is Ok, Cupid Weekly

JOY BUZZER

An Extended Limerick About the Clitoris AKA a Climerick

There once was a man who was sure
His cock was a kind of a cure
He seemed unprepared
When his lover declared
That his love making was hit or miss
The answer dear sir, is the Clitoris
This poem is a lie
There's way more than one guy
In fact, I would say there are millions more.

PRIME CUTS

Every time I go thru airport security
despite their pervy x-ray glasses,
my belly gets an intimate blue-gloved rub down.
They say, I *alarmed in that area*
but don't I always?
Perhaps I should submit a butcher's diagram of all the things they
might find in my fat.

The upper left quadrant is primarily
made up of inconsequential things:
swallowed bubblegum and the hearts of my enemies.

The bottom left IS actually made up of snack cakes
suspended in feelings,
a jello mold of angst and sugar.
If you are trying to find my shame it should be there
somewhere but there are better things blocking the way.

A humble museum of loves lost and kept
occupies the upper right portion.
There is a gift shop full of stuff former lovers have left behind.
it really is a must see.

The bottom right is where all of my awesome is stored.
It looks like an illegal fireworks trailer—
if you jostle it too much there will be a loud
and beautiful explosion.
This is where I get all of that confidence
you so are perplexed by,
the very thing that likely sounded the alarm.

The fucks I give about what anyone thinks
of my terrifying body

are all stored in my belly button.
Notice how it is an empty bowl waiting to be filled.

MY SUGAR, MY SWEET

You were baking a magnificent cake
3 tiers of white buttercream
Enough to share with all our friends
You said all you needed was a little more sugar
You went to the neighbors to borrow a cup
And did not come back for 3 days
When you finally crawled into bed
You slept thru Thanksgiving
All winter you ran next door
For sugar, you said
For us, you said
That magnificent cake, you said, *just needed a little more sugar*
It would all be so perfect if I would *just trust* you
If I would *stop asking so many fucking questions*

All your sweetness traded for sugar
When you tried to trade my sweetness too
I changed the locks
You moved into the apartment next door
Promised her our cake
Now the neighbor pours sugar into the bottomless cup where
Your nose used to be.

A GREEN BOOK FOR MY NIECE

For Kylie'a

You who was born with raw knuckles and open eyes
who sleeps arms crossed and angry because you already know.
There will be a day when you slip into your father's anger
like child feet into grown-man boots
you will stomp and scream and rage
and this rage will look foolish
except to us who also have black fathers.

There will be days you struggle with
knowing where you belong
for feeling like you belong everywhere
and nowhere at all.
There will be years when you feel bruised like worlds collided.
So, when they ask (and they always ask) what you are
tell them you are made up of whole worlds collided
supernova beautiful in its violent right to exist
violent like the night your white mother wrapped her privilege around
her knuckles
and reached thru the driver's side window of a woman who dared to
rename you something hateful and pulled back
without a single scratch and with a handful
of blonde hair writing an apology.
Remember this when you feel far from her
(and you will feel far from her).

Let no one tell you that you must choose a side
that you are more of one or too much of another.
Enough is a foul word.
You will learn to recognize hate thru its sugartooth smile
recognize whose heart is a sundown town.
You will learn to skin backhanded compliments down
to their racist bones and leave them for dead.
Be sure to tell them
that you are beautiful without conditions
that you are valid

that you are no one's token
no one's tragedy.
Tell them this in whatever tongue is most yours.
Code switching is an awful party
trick I hope you never have to learn.
Remember that the opposite of passing is not failing.
The opposite of passing is overcoming.
The opposite of passing is permanence.
You aren't going anywhere.
We aren't going anywhere.
We fight too hard to exist.
Go ahead and show them the ways you collide
like you were born from it.

PROMISSORY

For Dez

We are far and away from the days we were homecoming queens of
the convenience store parking lot, fuel pump island girls who smelled
of candy and gasoline, we welcomed in the cars whose bass shook the
ground like furious dancing gods
and offered ourselves up to them
when we knew what our youth and cleavage and the
well-timed lick of a blow pop could get us,
but not yet what they would cost us.
We never bothered to read the promissory notes
we signed
to be young
and girls
and without curfew.
We assumed the terms to be ours.

We could not know what we would leave behind
in wandering naive from our hilltop
that we would come to know what it means
to be debt-full and woman
and still with no one calling us home.

What tribeless girls we were
when we stumbled upon one another
and got our heartstrings tangled
what a fortune of unbalance that pushed us together
that kept us tethered.
I thank the rumble gods for you
for your steadying arms in the darkness.

One of these days we'll scrape enough gas money
from the floor mats to run away
someplace where we don't have to wear this skin like bark.
Someplace where we will not spend
any more years piling on scabs
until we are crab-shelled laughter ghosts.

We will be unsalted hot pearls.
We will stand on a beach tasting a salt spray not made of tears and
Midwest wind after everyone else has gone to sleep.
We will peel down to the soft fruit
and for once it won't hurt
and for once it will be on our terms.

FIRST IMPRESSIONS

(a found poem made up of the opening messages from my OKcupid inbox)

Hi
Hi
Heyy
Hey
Hey
Hello there.
Whats up?
Hey gorgeous
Good morning sexy
Hello, you areverypretty
Care to chat gorgeous?
Your gorgeous
Hey gorgeous. You're really sexy.
Hey, think your pretty, chat sometime?
Hello Cutie...How are you doing?
Look at u such a sexy woman!
Nice and busty :-)
Yummy
U so sexy
Your eyes are seducing me
I love your curves, you're a real hottie
You got any other piercings ;-P
You are very pulchritudinous
would love to show you what I got
Could i possibly get you to be bad with me?
you should text me dirty things
I think I would like to strip down and cuddle up with you
what do you think of oral sex, or do you prefer to use ur hands?
Are you into pegging?
Do as daddy says
do you like married men
Fuck, I want it
want to have sex with you
I would love to eat that ass and pussy
Mmm. I want that thick pussy in my face.

What are you doing? you should be in bed by now...with me ;-)
You're pretty and OMG your figure is absolutely breathtaking!
You are unbelievably gorgeous. I am rendered speechless

HOW TO EAT YOUR FEELINGS: SELF DOUBT

You will need:

  -1 box of ice cream bars
  (I prefer dove bars but any ice cream bar on a stick will do)
  -1 vibrator
  -Extra batteries (just in case)
  -1 Prince album

Operate the vibrator with one hand.
Eat an ice cream bar with the other
while listening to the Prince Album.
Prince doesn't allow for doubt.
Orgasm.
Repeat as needed.

Feeds:
All of Your Haters

SOMETHING AFTER BORROWED

The first time you left for all of my wanting too much
I waited
as long as I could
before I filled the shoebox with
      our wedding,
             our home in Indiana,

                               and our
                           daughter with
                           mismatched eyes.

I buried
it
all
in the empty
         field

         that would soon become a large and busy gas station
across the street from the restaurant
            where we'd had our first awkward date that
      ended with us stumble-kissed and full of sunrises.

Our girl is 5 years old
              when you come back and ask
              for her.
              I can no more resurrect
              the mother hunger in me
              than I can reach thru the concrete
              and pull
              her
              out for you now.

PEACE OFFERINGS FOR THE GIRL
WITH HER BACK PRESSED AGAINST THE DOOR

A vase of seed-headed dandelions for the first time you tried to fly off the front porch but managed only a goose egg on your forehead

A heart-shaped box of assorted deadbolts for the night you were left home alone and the man from 3 doors down tried to get in and you blew out your vocal cords screaming until he went away

One hundred long-stemmed summers for the night Grandma tried to scrub the extra melanin from your skin in the bathtub

A piggy bank full of safe passages home for that time the man stopped and jerked off in front of you and Cassandra on your way home from school

A crown of golden fall leaves plucked from mid-air for the second time you tried to fly, launching from the top bar of the swing set and managed only a set of bruised knees and gravel set like precious stones into your palms

A bracelet of diamond-cut baby teeth for the night the neighbor boy raped you and your mother found him on top of you but still sent you to his house to be looked after while she was at work

A bouquet of wild gods for the one you stopped believing in after losing the only other girl in the 5th grade who spoke dewey decimal when her house caught fire and she went up like a rare first edition

A pair of lover's deft hands to remove the hurt like surfacing splinters that still haunt your skin from the years of torment by an older brother who was scared of the sight of blood unless it was yours

For the third time you tried to fly, this time piloting a pill bottle rocket ship but instead managed to remain an earthling, there is no appeasement but rather a parade for the sweet gravity that held you here to this planet like an imperfect mother to her chest.

BIG WOMEN

It always begins with the kind of stare I can feel,
as though the sun itself is trying to render my body to flame
then the attempt to catch my elusive eye
followed by the questions of my availability
I radiate disinterest so hard I pulsate
and still inevitably the lean in and the whisper comes
but I like big women
As though the password to a speakeasy and I should open up and
serve him all my unlicensed intoxicating wares
As though my *no* was not due to indifference
but the certainty that this prince of public transit could not possibly be
interested in me
Massive me
He likes big women?
And yet he's not been thrown a parade?!
Attention Passengers of the #2 East Bound Main Street Bus:
He likes big women!
He likes big women so I should take off my giant panties
fall to my fat knees on this very bus and service him
He likes big women and that is more important that my comfort
Tell me, what are the odds that I, a big woman,
get on a city bus with this man
who happens to like big women?!
The stars are at last aligning in my favor!!
Three cheers for the knight who wants the castle
despite her princess
Let us take this bus to the end of the line and start a new life
where I will birth his children
and when they ask wide-eyed
mommy how did you know daddy was the one?

I can say,

Well, he boldly fought thru my personal boundaries while I was just
trying to get home from work and told me
that he liked big women
as though this isn't the subtlest way to say—
take who will have you
because who else will possibly want you like that?

THE OPPOSITE OF UP

Hey Baby, did it hurt
when you fell from my expectations?

Aye Boo, you MUST be a library book
because I kept you longer than I should have
and now it's costing me.

Hey Sugar, you know what this broom is for?
Cleaning up the pieces of my life after you left and took the dog.

Do you have a band-aid?
Cause I scraped my knee falling for your bullshit.

Hey Sweetheart, are your legs tired?
Cause you've been running from commitment your whole life.

I bet I could guess your sign...
It's Dead End, isn't it?

Could someone call the fire department?
Cause you are a dumpster fire.

Baby, if you were a sandwich at McDonald's
you would be the McSpineless.

Hey Darlin', if I could rearrange the alphabet I would
put F and U together.

Baby, you must be a magician
because abraca-FUCKYOU.

Was your daddy a sewer worker?
Cause you are full of shit.

Hey Sugar, where ya goin'?
I hate to see you leave but I love watching you walk into traffic.

HOROSCOPE FOR THE PREMATURE SCORPIO: JULY 2014

That Sad-Eyed Boy you share this sign with
is a Midwest Speed Trap.

Apparently he does not know what he wants but it isn't you.
Apparently, you're amazing and all but it isn't you.
Today, you find your bursting heart again
in the house of too much.
Today it is okay to be angry and to want
these last three months back
to want a return on all that hope you spent so easily on this
too easily on this
Today, your teeth are full of jade and questions
with no point in asking.
Today, you hate him for what you were willing
to give up/trade/compromise
and for what he will not. It is okay to call out this cowardice.
In fact, go ahead and say things you cannot take back.
Fuck the consequences.
This was a mistake. You should not have come here.
This is a mistake. You should go away now.

Lucky Numbers: the miles between you, the 5 years between
breakups, and that one awkward time he thought you said
I Love You.

HAVISHAM

(inspired by Charles Dickens' *Great Expectations*)

I cannot consider it tomorrow until I have slept. I was to be a married
woman by this time tomorrow and as I have no husband now it cannot
be tomorrow. I will not sleep.
Midnight's arm is not strong enough to lift and turn the calendar day,
not with my sodden & angry heart resting atop it...I live this endless
and awful day, a punishment for believing I could be something other
than an empty house...
I've got an altar for a good promise...a set of gold-plated
picture frames for good pictures,
a string of moon-headed lanterns for a good party.
I've got this cake...this cake turned corpse flower, the flies devoured
the blooms and left the stench. I've got this vanishing groom for my
fool's heart. I've got this un-listening God for a wailing prayer. I've
got this echo feeding me back my own begging...I got this dress, o'
this dress...wouldn't be right to take it off now. A bride undoing her
own corset?! I am unconsummated. I was a beautiful bride. I would
have been a good wife, a happy home.
I towed myself across the threshold. I am the town's whisper fool,
jilted bride, foreclosed wife, forsaken home, tantrum at God's own
feet. It seems he will not make me an upright bride in this dress so I
should marry the dirt. Lord, send me a man
to wring my neck or take my hand
truly, send me a man who is not as silent as God is to me now and I
will worship him.

I SPENT YEARS NOT WEARING RED BECAUSE BOLD COLORS ON BIG GIRLS
DRAW ATTENTION
AND GOOD GIRLS DO NOT WANT ATTENTION
BUT ANYWAY I AM FAT
AND THEREFORE INCAPABLE OF GOODNESS

So the dress will be red

like the first time you bleed thru the back of your skirt, red fabric,
spun from the cling of an unashamed lover on a crowded street and
just as soft as their lips there are pockets made of the attic crawl
spaces of old homes for your brass knuckles and your lipstick and
photos of your grandmother feeling bold in her bikini in 1964

and it is strapless

and it can be strapless because the bust line is made from the branches
of pomegranate trees and the backbone of Atlas but with an underwire
made of the weightlessness felt in water the dress flares at the bottom
like a mermaid tail

made of fireworks

and wish-headed dandelions. The whole thing stitched with string
lights pulled straight from a Christmas tree holding

everything you ever coveted

but were denied for not being deemed worthy piled underneath
because we are worthy of wanting this dress doesn't ask for
attention

it takes

it.

LETTER TO MY CAT, EXPLORING MY IMPENDING SPINSTERHOOD

(After Andrea Gibson)

Dear Clementine

Aka Clemmy
Aka Russian Ballet Legend Clemerushka
Aka Oh My Darlin' Oh My Darlin' Oh My Darlin' Clementine
Aka My Fat Bottomed Girl
Aka My Side Eye With Fur and Four Legs
I read somewhere that cats nuzzle their faces against things
to claim them as their own.
Everything in our apartment belongs to you,
including me.
I know you think it's dumb that I only sleep 6-8 hours
one time per day,
that there is anything that requires me to be anywhere other than
where you can heavily drape yourself across my hip
like a lover's arm
or curl into the big spoon of my body
like a dollop of marmalade.
For the record I think it's dumb too
but someone's gotta pay the rent and you won't
even put a resume together.
At the job I leave you to go to each day there is a terrible man
who says that he hates cats because
your affection has to be earned.
He says this like it is a bad and impossible thing.
He also thinks it's perfectly acceptable to whistle in the office
so it's not like he has any real credibility anyway
but his seems to be a popular opinion.
I know it must seem strange that I would ever come running
the first or fifth or twelfth time someone calls my name
but some nights I wake up from a dead sleep feeling so alone
and I just need to know you're still around
and even when you are busy with the important duty
of stalking a moth on the living room wall
I appreciate that you do eventually come.

I really like the way you hate basically everyone except me
especially on the days I am convinced
everyone else actually does hate me.
There are days I hate everyone except you.
There are never days that I hate you though
not even when you claw the furniture
not even when you wake me up on Saturday mornings to
alert me that your food bowl isn't all the way full, but
only part of the way full and that this is unacceptable.
I like the way you don't settle for less.
My mom says it is a sign that you are comfortable and happy when
you lay on your back and show me your tummy.
This is a love language I understand.
The last person I got comfortable enough to lay on my back
and show my tummy to was a man I loved so much that I
want to vomit in his absence the same way you vomit when
you think I have been gone for an unreasonable amount of
time. This man has been gone an unreasonable amount of time
and if he is gone for good this relationship will have ended
no differently than any other failed relationship
you've witnessed over these last 11 years
and this makes me think about how long it took you
to stop smooshing stink bugs.
I think love might be my stink bugs

Clem,

I've got no more prowl left in me to bring anyone
home who doesn't
see the worth in earning my affection.
Or who doesn't occasionally wake up just to make
sure that I am still here.
The spinster trope goes that we should grow reclusive
and brittle together,
until one morning you'll come to alert me
of your not entirely full bowl
to find me rigid and begin nibbling at the

drying skin of my fingertips.
Wouldn't that be a luxury,
to not have to witness you leaving me also
to never find that you've slunk off to the basement,
curled up behind a box of Christmas decorations
and betrayed me with the shuttering of your heart
leaving me here,
belonging to no one

WHAT IS LEFT

(For my Grandma)

The doctor said it could be malignant
the gumball mass removed from your jawline
radiation to let it know it is not welcome back here.

And then you discover that your taste buds are a valley
of dead radio waves
not a dance to be had on your arid tongue
until, like an overlooked present found when taking down
the Christmas tree
a lucky unscathed tulip after the bomb smoke clears
one lone tower filling the silent dark with the best song—

     Chocolate.
You can still taste chocolate.
You can actually only now taste chocolate
a love note from God that he sees you and he
remembers the little things
a communion in Hershey squares
breakfasts of fudge swirled, double-scooped envy
a wealthy lover buying dinner every night.
Your tongue is a golden ticket that Charlie Bucket
would run thru the streets for.
You're pretty sure you wished for this once
in childhood at the malt shop,
which has long ago stopped being a malt shop,
when your father leaned down and told you that
you could have whichever flavor you wanted
and everything is malt shop now
because you said
     Chocolate.

A LITANY ON BREATHING

For D.P.

You are mopping up your mother again
and holding your breath
You are learning how to take a punch
and holding your breath
You are not living up to your potential
You are skipping school again
You are dropping out
and holding your breath
You are broken water 3 times
First for a serious blue-eyed boy coated in apologies who
will understand all of this one day
Then to a school of angry minnows in the shape of a little brown girl
who knows too much
and whose father reminds you how to take a punch
Last to a son with moth-wing eyelashes and a mouth full of light
bulbs whose father is lost in the sofa cushions again
and you are still holding your breath
You go to work when it is dark
and come home when it is dark
and you are holding your breath
The phone is jangling, an aggressive beggar's cup
The children have eaten the plates and filled the sink with snapping
turtles
There is sand in the carpet
The windows are cracking from water pressure
and you are holding your breath
On the night you are pulled over in a swerving car
full to the roof with river water
You wish the officer could see how good you have been
at holding your breath
and holding your breath
and holding your breath
and holding
You are sure that this is the time you will turn blue
That the blood damming in your eyes will burst to hemorrhaging until

it is dark
That the seams of your lungs will rip like overstuffed plastic grocery
bags when your hands are already full
That you do not have one more push off from bottom left in Your
concrete legs

And then, instead,
you sprout gills.

FOR MY GRANDPA ON HIS 76TH BIRTHDAY

Today I am wearing your watch faces like trustier knee caps
I am eating peanut butter straight from the jar
and I am letting the rage blossom in me
like a sickness of dahlias

Later,
I will hurl a loaded dinner plate against the wall
I will name things unfair and complain to the moon
I will sneak down to the basement to eat ice cream
like the sweetest mistress
whom I was told to give up
like I wasn't going to die a cursed man anyway.

NO ONE'S

I stand at the very edge of my yard clicking my tongue to the backs of my teeth and making low coaxing sounds in the hope that at best it is resting and at worst it is just injured, that this beckoning to the dog on the curb will stir some sign of life. The flies starting to congregate do not muster even an ear flick and I already know but I won't step off my property line, because in this spot I cannot see the dog's face and without seeing the dog's face I can entertain hope. I consider the swollen belly, bloat so soon? Or was there a handful of blind possibilities also now dead?

I call my mother to ask
who one contacts to
collect no one's dead dog.
She says that the dead dogs
she has handled have all
been her own, the ones
she has carried upstairs
when their hips got too weak
or whose mouths she has
spooned baby food into
when their kibble became
too exhausting, each one
of them ushered with
loving strokes to their loyal
and domestic fur towards
a sleepy death,
nothing so violent,
so sudden as this dog
someone hit and left on the curb
in front of my house

this dog I am trying to will the rise and fall of a flank out of,
just one shallow breath from, some flicker that I am wrong,
some sign to unglue me from this spot
and send me down to the curb,
to reach out, and have my hand met with something warm,
something I could comfort or at very least
for the ability to blink,

to turn my head, long enough for the dog to be spirited away
by some means that will allow me to believe that it got up

                                                 and
                                            went home
                                            where it is
                                            loved.

WHEN WE WERE KINGS, ONE DAY

When my niece is 4 years old
she stands on her chair in a Wendy's
to give me lessons on how to roar like a lion.
She shows me how she pulls the sound up from her feet
gnashes her teeth
a smear of ketchup turned gazelle's blood
at the corner of her mouth
tells me, *Girls can be Kings too!*
She is making her fiercest lion face
when a man walks up and tells her to smile,
that *she is too pretty to have her face all screwed up like that.*
And she obliges,
but she does so as a lion
with still-twitching prey clamped in her jaws.
She locks eyes with him and growls until he walks away.
King of the Jungle is she.

Now my niece is 6 and skipping pizza day because she
all of a sudden worried
if she's thin enough to be a queen
or just pretty enough to be someone's trophy.
The tallest girl in her class stoops
from being told to make herself smaller
smiles mouth closed to hide missing teeth,
not to show imperfection
swallows the right answers in class, not to look too smart.
She is being tamed for the poachers and I am undone.
I see you, Patriarchy.
You gas leak, you pickpocket, you wasps nest
in the attic, you virus of glass,
you hothouse minefield.
I see the 2 short years it took you to hollow her
defiance into something ungainly.
I have already spent too much of my reign
a circus act of obedience
with your head too close to my teeth.
You will not have her too.

This is the notice of your dismantling.
I will split wide the bellies of men who have
plundered us for our growl,
build stilts out of the femurs of men
who expect us to shrink for them
and stack crowns worthy of only girl kings out of the teeth
of men who tell women to smile.
We are coming for what is ours
and we all will be kings again, one day.

HOW TO EAT YOUR FEELINGS: LONELINESS

You will need:

> -Your prom dress (if it still fits) or some other formal wear
> -1 OkCupid account
> -1 jar of Trader Joe's Cocoa Swirl Cookie Butter

Get dressed up like it's prom night and your whole young glamourous
life is still ahead of you. Eat the cookie butter. Straight from the jar.
Surf OkCupid. Weep hard and ugly
at the options laid before you.
Pass out in your formal wear,
your face mascara streaked
and chocolate smeared.

Feeds:
That Gaping Abyss in Your Heart because

ANOTHER one of your Facebook friends just got engaged and you
will likely die alone with no one noticing your body for weeks or
even months because you have become somewhat of a shut-in these
last couple of years, how could you possibly expect to meet anyone
this way?

FORM LETTER TO MY EXES TO PREPARE THEM
FOR AN ONCOMING PLAGUE OF GIRLS WHO WERE JUST SO SURE

Greetings <Enter Applicable Ex's Name Here>

You are receiving this letter because at one point in time you dated one, Rachel C Wiley. She may or may not have told you she loved you. You may or may not have broken her heart. Regardless she at one point thought you were "the one" and the whole thing probably ended very badly.

It has come to our attention that after an accident in a lab there has been a recent outbreak of former Rachels. Writhing up thru the ground after 17 years like a swarm of fresh cicadas,
covered in the dirt of heartbreaks long passed.
There is a chance that one or more of these Rachels
might still think you are "the one."
There is a chance that she thinks she can
"fix things" between you.
There is a chance she is on her way to you right now.
Perhaps one has already appeared to you,
in her prom dress on your parents' lawn,
or waving an outdated cellphone full of thirty-five-cent-apiece text message love proclamations,
or stuffing small cardboard Valentine's Day cards into a shoebox she attached to your desk at your place of employment.
Things are going to get awkward.
Should you encounter one of these shell-skinned Rachels we ask that you contact us immediately with her current whereabouts. You may approach the Rachel to try to keep her in one place but try to avoid eye contact as these former Rachels
do take this as a sign of affection.
In the event that you have already re-rejected a Rachel and she is standing in front of your home scream singing *I Have Nothing* by the late great Whitney Houston* and holding up photoshopped renderings of what your children might have looked like please advise your lovely wife and children to stay indoors. The heartbroken Rachel can be lured into a shed or garage with a jar of Trader Joe's Cocoa Swirl Cookie Butter.

Once inside you may barricade the door and contact us for removal. If your Rachel is from the early 2000s she may be soothed into an angsty vegetative state with any Fiona Apple album and a box of wine.

Finally, we cannot stress enough that the women before you do not represent the current state of Rachel C Wiley's heart. The real-time Rachel C Wiley is, in fact, long over you.**

Kindest Regards,
The International Bureau of Unresolved Feelings

*Footnote 1: The Rachel duplicate is likely unaware of the death of Whitney Houston. Please refrain from adding this crushing blow to the bad news that you do not love her, it might be more than she can take.

**Footnote 2: Though if you are still by chance single she might be interested in seeing if any of those old feelings still exist, perhaps over dinner.

EXPECT-CUM PATRONUS

Another Climmerick

3 out of 4 women attest
for orgasms penetration is not best
with a swish and a flick
with your tongue, not your dick
you'll be a wizard in bed
for giving good head
and shoulder above all the rest!

DRY CAKE WISHES AND TAP WATER DREAMS

On the birthday of the ex-boyfriend who told me
I was "too intense"

I wish him a lifetime swaddled in beige, skinless chicken
boiled, Kraft singles, steamed rice, and unflavored oatmeal.
I wish him a wardrobe of Polo shirts—tucked in.
I wish him sex, but only ever in the bedroom
always lights out and socks on and planned in advance.
I wish him safety scissors and mayonnaise
and the entire state of Indiana.
I wish him not exactly love but a like that could be mistaken
for love on a slightly overcast day.
I wish him slightly overcast days
and lukewarm showers, Saltine Crackers and skim milk.
I wish him a prefab house in the suburbs painted in
colors that resemble unflavored oatmeal.
Unsalted butter. One-ply toilet paper. The music
of Mumford and Sons.
A commute to work in colors that resemble unflavored
oatmeal to a job that requires him to wear polo shirts—tucked in.
I wish him a windowless office,
Plain Cheerios never Honey Nut,
turkey bacon which is neither as good as turkey nor bacon.
I wish him crustless white bread sandwiches so he may
never know that the bread saw the joyful heat of an oven.
I wish him Great Clips haircuts, half-mast erections,
and engagement photos in an apple orchard.
I wish him a wedding in a strip mall chapel wearing his
very best polo shirt—tucked in.
I wish him a wife that wears headbands for function
and never for fashion
who gives him halfhearted lube-less hand jobs and a
pair of dress socks for every anniversary.
I wish him a golden retriever that pees in the exact same
spot on the carpet—not every day
but just often enough that he forgets and steps in
it in socked feet on a Wednesday morning.

I wish a week of Wednesday Mornings.
I wish him a lifetime of safety and platitudes,
a soundtrack of florescent lights humming.
I do not wish him me any longer, though.
Never me again.
I do wish him all of the children he said
he was not sure he wanted,
including and especially a daughter, whose eyes remind
him far too much of mine.

REJECTION #3

Dear MikeTheRaidersFan,

Thank you for your submission: *I know you won't message me back but I just wanted to say that your beautiful*

but unfortunately the submission deadline for faux self-effacing reverse psychology closed in 2004 when we stopped waiting to be told we were pretty and got busy giving hand jobs to confident men.

Regretfully, you are not reading this rejection because self-fulfilling prophecy is a bitch we have drinks with every Friday during happy hour.

Good luck in finding a home for your cock.

Kindest Regards,
You Cannot Get into My Pants Without Knowing the Difference Between Your and You're Weekly

(A subsidiary of Nothing Is Ok, Cupid Quarterly)

JOYCE CAROL VINCENT: ILLUSIONIST

In 2003, 38-year-old Joyce Carol Vincent died in her London apartment. Her
death and body went unnoticed for nearly 3 years.

There are 3 parts to every illusion.

First, the Pledge: Do you know this woman?
Have you seen her before?
She is an ordinary single woman.
She is placed in a simple home.
She lives there alone
The doors and windows all locked
Normal locks
The same as you and I have on our homes.
You can check them yourselves.
No trap doors, no smoke and mirrors.
Are you watching closely?
Have I mentioned she is alone?
Single?
Watch closely.

Second, the Turn: and just like that, one day, she is gone.
Could be anywhere,
in time you do not even notice.
And she could be everywhere.
You might try to remember when it was you saw her last.
But she is long gone without being gone
The doors and windows still locked
The same as you and I have on our homes.
You can check them yourselves.
Were you watching closely?
A large fat crow released from her palm.
Abra Cadaver.

Third, the Prestige:
The illusion is a success when they're all asking how it's done
A disappearing so unconcealed
An escape so mundane

Lock picker, knot worker, halter of time
The 3-year holding of breath
Before they discovered her remains.
She was still infinitely alive and everywhere.
Could have been anywhere.
Do you know this woman?
Have you seen her before?
Were you watching closely?
She is an ordinary single woman
The doors and windows all locked
Normal locks
The same as you and I have on our homes
The same as I have on my home.
You can check them yourselves.
Did I mention she was alone?
Did I mention I live alone?
Will you check them yourselves?
Will you check on me?
Watch
Closely.

Please,
Don't let me disappear
Too.

SLEEPING GIANTS

For Leo, For Myself, For Anyone who has ever been too big to be seen

There are so many stories that demand the giant must be felled
that the small are righteous and deserving of all they can
take from the massive beast
that all the golden things are up for grabs
that the riches must've been ill-gotten to begin with
You colossus
You behemoth
You titan
You who can shoulder the very earth
who are you to alter this narrative?
They're already looking for ways to discredit regular survivors
You make it too easy
Your body, its own defamation
They'll say you are too big to have been raped
That victim is not a shirt that comes in your size
They'll laugh at the idea of you being overtaken
say you are too much mountain for anyone to move
They'll say you have so much weight to place behind your No
say one flick of your massive wrist would've brought
the whole thing to a stop
They'll say that you must have wanted it
That in fact, you are a monster of wanting
your mammoth body laid out as evidence
for the way it feasts so greedily on the space around it
They'll say you stand a lighthouse of untruth
in search of attention
a bitter leviathan,
and anyone who toppled you earned that conquering,
that they must be a knight, an Argonaut,
a future king coming for your severed head
Your truth sounds too much like thunder
frightens the whole village
frightens them into taking up torches and pitchforks
a swarm to chase you to the edge of the cliff
a mob come to tether you to the earth to pluck out your eyes
for what they refuse to see

They'd sooner pry open your mouth for the gold fillings
than take your word
that you were but a sleeping giant
who was not awakened nor deemed worthy
for something golden as consent.

SPOILAGE

Your sweetest love asks to borrow some silence
& as if on cue all of the forgotten hurts, preserved
in previous canning seasons,
begin to erupt in the cellar.
Every lidded mouth full & pickled with insecurity gives
over to the swell of rancid things
pushed into the dark for much too long,
an exorcism of jarred ghosts,
an oozing display of fireworks coating the walls in a
layer of vinegary mistrust.
As you apologize for the noise & promise to keep this
messy doubt from sullying the peace you've promised
them, an especially potent wound rockets thru the floorboards
trailing a comet of sour molasses & lands
on your patient love's lap
still whistling from the pressure.

HOW TO EAT YOUR FEELINGS: ANXIETY
(FROM BEING TRAPPED IN A DEAD-END DAY JOB AND NEVER FULFILLING YOUR POTENTIAL, PROVING ALL OF THE JERKS FROM HIGH SCHOOL RIGHT)

You will need:

    -To have eaten M&Ms somewhat recently
    -Cleavage

When you find the errant M&M in your cleavage (because there is always at least one) consider it as you would a cyanide capsule that could end all of your suffering, right now.
Eat it.
Slowly.
Let the hard candy shell melt like so much
hope in a windowless office.
When it does not kill you—consider this your new lease on life. Take the rest of the day off work. Go to the park. Eat a gyro from a cart. Feel the wind in your hair and the sun on your face. Commune with nature (unless there are birds nearby. Fuck birds.)
Pretend you never have to go back to work.

Feeds:
One Cubicle-Damaged Soul.

SOLIDARITY WITH MISS COLOMBIA 2015

(after the host of the 2015 Miss Universe competition, Steve Harvey,
crowned Miss Colombia, Ariadna Gutiérrez, the winner in error)

And they will talk about how gracefully she stood there
while the crown was plucked from her head
just as she felt the satisfying weight of it resting on her skull
they will call her strong but she did not come here to be strong
there are means to strength that are not heartbreak
he said the universe was hers
until he said it wasn't.

SETTLE

So maybe one day I'll just settle
in a pastel senior citizens' home
my life reduced to what can fit onto a dresser top,
a life raft.
Some nice man and I will bond over the side effects of
our blood pressure pills
and then just settle in together like ribs after a deep sigh.
He will absent-mindedly call me by his dead wife's name.
I will turn down my hearing aids.
He will have the best hard candies in the whole joint.
I will quietly hope to die first so as not to be left again.
His children will politely hate me,
bringing nice though impersonal gifts at Christmas.
It'll be fine.
Just fine.

THEY BOLT THE HEADBOARDS TO THE WALLS THESE DAYS

Last night at a Days Inn next to a highway on-ramp
in small-town Ohio we were "those people,"
the howling inconsiderates of room 126 who made
the travelers in the rooms on either side and above of us
turn their televisions up,
made the traveling businessmen uncomfortable
in their double beds
        the trucker longs for someone warm
        the arguing couple pause and laugh and remember when they
        were "those people"
and because none of them banged on the wall
or complained to management
I wish them the very best sleep of their lives tonight
because I cannot and would not
give them back last night.

A RESPONSE TO THE MEN OF OKCUPID ADAMANT ABOUT SHOWING ME THEIR COCKS

I.

I do not wish to see your dick on cam
Nor on Tinder or Instagram
I could not would not on a phone
Nor on an iPad, please leave me alone
I do not wish to see your cocks
Not in your hands, nor in a box
I will not see it on a boat
Or side-by-side with the TV remote
I would not could not watch you jerk it online
Not on YouTube, FetLife, or Vine
Not on GChat, Tumblr, or Kik
No, I do not wish to see your dick.

II.

A Working List of Places I WOULD Like to See Your Dick:
   • Thrusting towards the spin of a rusty fan blade

PARADISE

I promise
I have tried every method the body zealots insist
will make me worthy
the loathing
the withholding
the pain
the castigation
the flagellation
the suppression
the obey
obey
obey
and still
I am this feral landscape
an orchard of gluttonous fruit trees
and was cast from the paradise of my body by the shame gods
banished from reveling in my own flourish
rolling hills
secret valleys
the tree-trunk thighs
heavy sugar-apple breasts
I am sick for the springs I missed while exiled into my head
as though a country separate from fleshy hips
It cost me years of knowing my own clay
and now that I have clawed my way back into this Eden
I intend to bask
O', I intent to feast.

ODE TO ALL THE MOTHERS I BORROWED

There were years I spent wandering the west side of Columbus, a
sharp-tongued girl in too much eyeliner and flannel shirts from the
men's section that were only outsized by my too-many, messy
feelings

Your children brought me to your doorsteps
a found and muddy thing
And you made space for me in your homes,
at your tables, in your plans
Me with swear words stuck between my teeth
Me, feral and ready for a fight
Me, chipped nail polish and crying in your bathrooms

You,
returning me to my own home as late as you could because
you caught the confessions I draped in crass jokes
You, seeing the unmothering in my fingernails
chewed to the quick
what a ghost town I would have been without you
what a collection of unfocused photographs
what a loss

WAITING FOR THE END OF THE WORLD

Every spring before I fell in love with you
I inevitably found a dead robin at my feet.
As robins mate for life I took this as some sad omen
of another lonely year
and when you did leave I was certain
red-breasted birds would drop at my feet from the sky like blood
sticky teeth from God's own mouth.
I read once that losing teeth in dreams is a subconscious
fear of losing one's beauty.
It has been 2 years.
So far the road is still not paved with crimson feathers.

So far you are still gone.

So far I am still beautiful.

FOR FAT GIRLS WHO CONSIDERED STARVATION WHEN BULIMIA WASN'T ENOUGH

Mom says that my teeth are perfect.
Perfect brother has just gotten braces on his top four front teeth
a tiny railroad bridge connecting nothing
and mom says that my teeth are perfect.
At last my quiet mouth, the overlook, the swallowed
feelings have all paid off
and cultured something perfect
and mine.
My mouth is a music box
stuffed with pearls.

Perfect brother is tall
and lean
eats whatever he wants.
One time a whole box of oatmeal cream pies.
But it is clearer each day that my baby fat
is no longer baby fat
but just fat.
It is clearer each day that I will not be a ballerina.
I had wanted to be a ballerina.
My mouth is a music box.
A small girl spins gracefully at the back of my throat
on point.
I am sure if I can just reach far enough back I could still
have her grace.
I reach for her every night after dinner while the bathtub fills.

Until one day the health teacher shows us a photo
of a mouth crammed full of broken, yellowed dishes
says that a side effect of Bulimia
is ruined teeth
but Mom said that my teeth were perfect.
And my perfect is a ransom I cannot bring myself to pay
for the spinning girl

so I swallow her
and then nothing more for 4 whole days.
My mouth is a music box,
plays a low gear grinding that puts me to sleep.

When I do not wake up any closer to the spinning girl
encircled in pink tulle
but rather still a ravenous hollow encircled in overgrowth
I sneak down to the pantry and devour an entire box of
oatmeal cream pies in the dark
before going upstairs to brush my perfect teeth one at a time.

THE LEAVING

For Ben

If I get to be old, my body a tower of carelessly stacked dishes in polyester slacks that somehow makes it from breakfast to dinner and to breakfast once again without celebrating a milk-glass confetti onto the ground, my hair a wild bouquet of television antennas, my eyes a pair of bashful blue brides hiding behind ivory veils, my skin a well-traveled and sinking hot air balloon

If I begin to stand on the back porch and call in for dinner a cat that was found curled under the porch in a peaceful rest long before my teeth were pulled and replaced with ill-fitting typewriter keys that click and ding and must be slid back into place, I hope that my hermit-crab brain crawls up and into the memory of this thing between us that is love but not need

I will call the mailman by your name and swoon over the gifts you bring me each day

Every grocery list, a love letter scrawled to you until my hands fuse into conch shells I can only press to my ears to feel the hum of all of the kisses blown from and caught in my palms
and in this way even the leaving will be beautiful
as beautiful as that evening I flew back home alone and untouched
but never more sure that I loved you

The city, your city, that I love in the same way that I love you disappearing

a closing mouth full of gold teeth in the heavy-headed sun resting nestled on the clouds like a lover's chest.

HOW MY FEMINISM LEARNED TO TALK

Its first word was predictably

No.

The neighbor boy has a growth spurt this summer
the wrestling becomes not wrestling
the point no longer to pin and tickle,
or to test strength and Houdini escapes
but now only to pin down and take.

At the park one afternoon,
you see yourself in the reflection of the hot metal slide
as he presses you against it
you see yourself the way he must see you in that moment
as though the subject of a photograph cropped at the neck
and your mouth instinctively deploys a flare
in hopes that he will return your head.

You shut your eyes and see a galaxy of flares
that he will never know,
and wake up aware of a new world
where you are simply told not to wear dresses to
the park anymore
and you push past the ash smoldering in your new
woman mouth to say
that it is not the dress
but the boy's hands that should be removed.

BELLY KISSES

There is a beautiful woman in my bed.
After a lot of awkward flirting
we started kissing on my couch
then made our way up to my bedroom,
auxiliary articles of clothing
(cardigans, leggings, socks) peeling away
until all that remains between our skins are our simple dresses.
My first instinct any time my dress is pulled over my head
is to wrap my arms across my belly
less in shame
and more a shield from the disgust the world
constantly promises for it
I love my body more days than I don't and that is a long-
won battle,
but asking anyone else to love my body still sometimes
feels like asking too much.
Every time I've let someone fuck me with my dress still on
I laid in bed afterwards
and vowed that I would not let another person inside me
that hasn't seen me fully—not just seen but marveled at
and pressed their lips to the parts deemed unworthy
a promise I break every time the need to be touched
outweighs the need for dignity.
I am still learning how to ask for what I deserve without it
also sounding like an apology.
When at last I hold my breath and plunge from my
dress into open air
there is a beautiful woman waiting on the other side,
and unasked she presses her lips to my belly
before I can reach to cover it.
And she marvels,
And she runs her hands over all of me like her palms
might just slough the world's cruelty from my skin
There is this beautiful woman in my bed
and she holds beauty the same way I hold beauty
hard won with both hands, overflowing
When she emerges from the poly/cotton undertow

of her own dress
how can I help but love her body the same way
I have fought every day to love my own?
And now I kiss, I marvel, I reach
& her body answers my wanting hands
She is endless
We are both so endless and unshielded
and weightless here
in my bed
Weightless
but not the least bit smaller
thank God not the least bit smaller

BURYING MY HUSBAND

You sure have slept with a lot of husbands
to never be anyone's wife

and at first this loneliness feels something like karma.
The wedding dream once dense as a tower of cake

stacked 4 tiers high and iced with buttercream is suddenly cultured down
into a hard, sharp sliver on the tongue.

You can remember how the dream still loomed

that time you binge watched "Say Yes to the Dress"
with your ex-boyfriend

while he grinded his teeth and asked to borrow money.
And it was still there on your 31st birthday when nothing
at all exceptional happened.

No one sending flowers to your cubicle for the
office ladies to coo over.

No one else as excited about this day as you.

You know it lingered at Christmas last year when,
alone and drunk on spiked cider,

you locked yourself in the bathroom clutching an
arrangement of makeup brushes
and pink daisy razors,

a toilet paper train tucked into your pantyhose
while you wept thru three tubes of the good mascara.

But then,

you woke up one day as though the first day of some 5th season
starfished in the middle of your queen-size bed

and rolled around in the consideration that you owe
to absolutely no one

on whether or not to get up and do the dishes or spend half
the day in bed browsing the Ikea catalog for a duvet cover

for which only your opinion matters before getting up and knowing that
there are takeout leftovers

from the night before
that no one else has eaten

or taking a shower knowing all of the hot water
is yours for the taking and it all feels like some kind of great love story;

You + last night's Lo Mein

You + an obscenely floral duvet

You + all of this lavish space

You + all of this delicious silence

You + this in-ground pool
of non-obligation to anyone at all.

THANKS & ACKNOWLEDGMENTS

Thank you to Sam and Dylan and the team at Button Poetry for giving this book a home. Thank you Hanif Abdurraqib for saying yes to editing this book and for being a constant and breathing reminder that Columbus, Ohio is a good place to call home.

Unmeasurable Love and Thanks to my Pink Door Coven for nurturing my magic even when I think it is gone, especially Rachel McKibbens and the whole family, for always holding a space that I can run away to.

Special thanks to my friends and chosen family, that I could not do any of this without: Hope Hill, William Evans, Dave Nichols, Siaara Freeman, Alex & Karen Scott, Ben Figueroa, and Denise Jolly.

I am endlessly grateful to my bestest, Desiree Pipenger, for knowing everything about me and loving me still and harder than anyone and also for letting me be Aunt Rach to her children.

To my loves Shelly Haynes & Abi Bechtel ; thank you for your patience with my stunted and frightened feelings. Thank you for being a soft place for me to land at the end of the process that was writing this book.

Acknowledgements:

"Paradise," "But They Say I Will Not Make It," "Mixed Girl," "Spoilage," "Sleeping Giants," "My Whiteness Hits On Me in a Bar," and "Femme Visibility" were all previously published in the 2017 QTPOC edition of *Crab Fat Magazine*.

Versions of "Glory in Two Parts," "For Fat Girls Who Considered Starvation When Bulimia Wasn't Enough," and "To the Girl in Blackface on Halloween 2011" were published in *Drunk In A Midnight Choir* in 2015.

ABOUT THE AUTHOR

Rachel Wiley is a performer, poet, feminist, and fat positive activist from Columbus, Ohio. Rachel has represented Columbus at multiple National Poetry Slam competitions. She has toured nationally performing at slam venues, colleges, and festivals. Her work has appeared on *Upworthy*, *The Huffington Post*, *The Militant Baker*, *Everyday Feminism* and *PBS News Hour*. Her first poetry collection, *Fat Girl Finishing School*, was published in 2014 by Timber Mouse Publishing.

OTHER BOOKS BY BUTTON POETRY

If you enjoyed this book, please consider checking out some of our others, below.
Readers like you allow us to keep broadcasting and publishing. Thank you!

Aziza Barnes, *me Aunt Jemima and the nailgun.*

J. Scott Brownlee, *Highway or Belief*

Nate Marshall, *Blood Percussion*

Sam Sax, *A Guide to Undressing Your Monsters*

Mahogany L. Browne, *smudge*

Neil Hilborn, *Our Numbered Days*

Sierra DeMulder, *We Slept Here*

Danez Smith, *black movie*

Cameron Awkward-Rich, *Transit*

Jacqui Germain, *When the Ghosts Come Ashore*

Hanif Willis-Abdurraqib, *The Crown Ain't Worth Much*

Aaron Coleman, *St. Trigger*

Olivia Gatwood, *New American Best Friend*

Donte Collins, *Autopsy*

Melissa Lozada-Oliva, *Peluda*

William Evans, *Still Can't Do My Daughter's Hair*

Rudy Francisco, *Helium*

Available at buttonpoetry.com/shop and more!